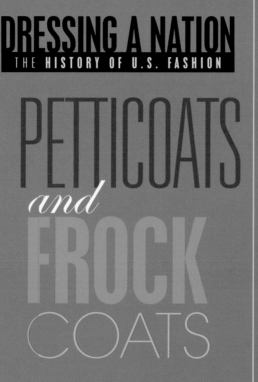

DRESSING A NATION
THE HISTORY OF U.S. FASHION

PETTICOATS
and
FROCK
COATS

Revolution and
Victorian-Age

FASHIONS
from the
1770s
to the 1860s

CYNTHIA
OVERBECK BIX

Twenty-First Century Books
MINNEAPOLIS

Dedication

To my wonderful husband, John, and son, Max, who support and encourage me in everything I do; and to my sister Deborah, my fellow writer and my best friend.
Special thanks to Peg Goldstein, whose keen editorial eye made this a better book.

Front cover image: A woman wears a skirt that splits open to reveal a petticoat in this late 1700s painting by William Williams.

Back cover image: This 1807 portrait shows a man wearing a frock coat and carrying a walking stick and top hat, popular fashions of the time for men.

Page 3 image: Martha Washington wears the fashions of the time, including mitts, a bonnet, and scarves, in the 1790s. Martha Washington was the wife of President George Washington.

Twenty-First Century Books
A division of Lerner Publishing Group, Inc.
241 First Avenue North
Minneapolis, MN 55401 U.S.A.

Website address: www.lernerbooks.com

Library of Congress Cataloging-in-Publication Data

Bix, Cynthia Overbeck.
    Petticoats and frock coats: Revolution and Victorian-age fashions from the 1770s to the 1860s / by Cythnia Overbeck Bix.
        p.   cm. — (Dressing a nation: the history of U.S. fashion)
    Includes bibliographical references and index.
    ISBN 978–0–7613–5888–6 (lib. bdg. : alk. paper)
    1. Clothing and dress—United States—History—18th century 2. Dress accessories—United States—History—18th century. 3. Fashion—United States—History—18th century. 4. United States—History—Colonial period, ca. 1600–1775. 5. United States—Social life and customs—To 1775. 6. National characteristics, American—History. I. Title
GT607.B59 2012
391.00973—dc22   2010053384

Manufactured in the United States of America
1 – MG – 7/15/11

CONTENTS

Couples dance the minuet in a ballroom in the 1700s. The women wear broad skirts that open in the front to reveal petticoats. The men wear rich frock coats and breeches, both made out of elegant fabrics such as silk.

Chapter One

NEW NATION, NEW CLOTHES

On an evening in the 1760s, in the ballroom of the Governor's Palace in Williamsburg, Virginia, wealthy men and women dance together with slow, stately steps to the music of violins. The women wear stiff, wide skirts, split in front to show richly embroidered petticoats, or underskirts. On their heads tower elaborate powdered hairdos. The men are dressed in elegant knee-length coats called frock coats, knee-length pants called breeches, white stockings, and buckled shoes. Jewels and satins glitter and gleam in the candlelight, and the air is heavy with perfume. These elegant people are dressed in the style of the French aristocracy—the source for all things fashionable in this era.

In colonial America (1600–1775), before the United States was a nation, scenes like this took place in the homes of wealthy and cultured merchants, government leaders, and plantation owners.

Then came the Revolutionary War (1775–1783), when the British colonies in North America fought for independence from Great Britain. After the war, American society began to change.

PLAIN AND SIMPLE

The men and women dancing at the Governor's Palace in Williamsburg were not typical colonial and Revolutionary-era Americans. These were the fashionable ladies and gentlemen whose fine clothes we see in painted portraits or preserved in museum collections. The women were ladies of leisure, with servants and dressmakers at their beck and call. The men were wealthy politicians, merchants, and plantation owners. They could hire tailors to dress them in the finest coats and breeches. These wealthy people made up less than 10 percent of the American population.

The majority of Americans in the late 1700s and early 1800s were middle class or poor. Most of them lived on farms or in small rural communities. Middle-class Americans tended small plots of land, ran village inns and shops, operated stables, and ran other small businesses.

HOMESPUN and Homemade

For the industrious, energetic laborers and farmers of the late 1700s and early 1800s, life was a daily round of hard work that left little time for frivolity. For women, that work included cooking, cleaning, and washing clothes by hand. It also involved spinning thread and yarn and stitching clothing for the whole family.

The homemade clothes worn by working people were not at all like the fine, tailor-made clothes of the wealthier classes. Nineteenth-century U.S. author Francis Underwood wrote, "A man whose clothes were made at home could be easily distinguished at a hundred yards' [91-meter] distance by his slouchy and baggy outlines," and women's dresses were "shaped without reference to elegance or fashion."

A woman rakes hay on a farm in the 1780s in this drawing by Francis Wheatley. Working women typically wore aprons over their dresses to keep them clean.

Because clothing was hard to make and expensive to buy, ordinary Americans had very few clothes. A farmer might have one outfit—a shirt, trousers, a vest, and a jacket—for winter and one for summer. For working in fields and driving teams of animals, some men wore long, full smocks over their clothes. To absorb sweat, they wore bandanas, or neckerchiefs.

A farm woman of this era might have just two or three dresses—one saved to wear as her Sunday best. Over her dress, she sometimes wore a boxy, loose-fitting jacket called a short gown. She added a triangular linen handkerchief around her neck and a linen cap over her hair. She tied an apron around her waist to catch dirt and keep her dress clean.

LABORER, SERVANT, SLAVE

The poorest class of laborers didn't own farms or shops. In rural areas, hired men worked for farmers, blacksmiths, stable owners, and village merchants. Women worked as servants, maids, cooks, laundresses, and seamstresses. Wages were low for all these workers. For the most part, they had only the clothes on their backs. These clothes were usually old mismatched hand-me-downs that needed constant mending. On her 1832 visit to Cincinnati, Ohio, then a very small city with dirt streets, British author Frances Trollope hired a young woman as a temporary servant. Trollope reported their conversation:

Seeing she was preparing to set to work in a yellow dress parsemé [sprinkled] with red roses, I gently hinted, that I

thought it was a pity to spoil so fine a gown and that she had better change it. "Tis just my best and my worst," she answered, "for I've got no other." And in truth I found that this young lady had . . . no more clothes of any kind than what she had on.

On the lowest rung of the social and economic ladder were African American slaves.

This woodcut depicts a blacksmith and a boy at a blacksmith workshop in 1789. Workingmen wore tough clothes that would hold up in sweaty and dirty workplaces.

This photo shows a family of field slaves picking cotton in Georgia in the 1860s. Slaves received only one or two outfits of rough clothing each year from the plantation master.

These men, women, and children worked as domestic servants in southern plantation homes or outdoors as field hands.

Field slaves had the shabbiest garments. They wore rough shirts, trousers, and dresses made of tow, a coarse kind of linen. Slave Charles Ball described one group working in the fields: "Each person had a coarse blanket, which had holes cut for the arms to pass through, and the top was drawn up round the neck, so as to form a sort of loose frock, tied before with strings." One slave owner posted a handbill, asking people to look out for a runaway slave named Lydia, probably a field hand. The flyer describes her as wearing "a white homespun habit [outfit] made of cotton and tow."

HOMESPUN *Revolt*

In the years leading up to the Revolutionary War, American women made some cloth at home. They spun sheep's wool into yarn, which they wove into woolen cloth. They spun cotton or flax fibers into cotton or linen thread. Women then wove the strands together to make cloth. Homemade wool or linen was known as homespun.

Homemade cloth accounted for only a small portion of fabric used in colonial America. Americans got most of their wool and other textiles from Great Britain. In fact, British laws said that Americans could not export their own wool and that fabrics imported to America had to arrive on British ships. The laws were designed to steer profits on fabrics to British merchants.

The colonists grew angry with British law. They didn't want to pay taxes to the British or support British merchants. Tensions grew between Britain and its American colonies.

HOW TO MAKE
HOMESPUN

The homespun fabric of the Revolutionary era was usually made of linen. This coarse but durable fabric came from the fibers of the flax plant (*above*). People grew the flax on their family farms. After harvesting, the flax stems were soaked in water, dried, and beaten with a heavy stick to separate the fibers from the wood. Next, the fibers were scraped, cleaned, and combed out in preparation for spinning. Women and girls spent long hours at the spinning wheel turning the flax fibers into thread. They spent more hours weaving the thread into cloth at a hand loom and finally stitching the cloth into garments.

Before the age of manufacturing, women spun their own yarn on a spinning wheel. In this 1700s illustration, a New England woman spins wool into yarn.

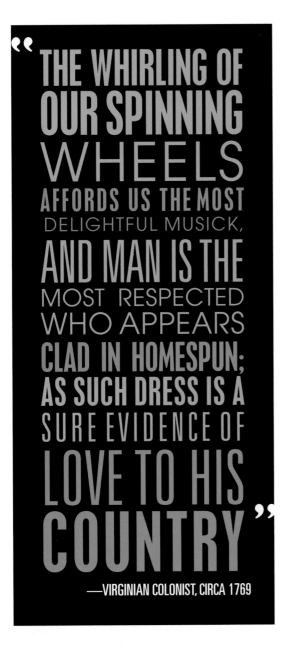

> **THE WHIRLING OF OUR SPINNING WHEELS AFFORDS US THE MOST DELIGHTFUL MUSICK, AND MAN IS THE MOST RESPECTED WHO APPEARS CLAD IN HOMESPUN; AS SUCH DRESS IS A SURE EVIDENCE OF LOVE TO HIS COUNTRY**
>
> —VIRGINIAN COLONIST, CIRCA 1769

In the 1760s, Americans began to boycott (refuse to buy) fabrics imported from Britain—along with other British goods. At first Americans boycotted only luxury items, such as lace, trim, and hats. Colonists also boycotted Chinese silks and Indian cottons, which arrived in America on British ships. Then Americans started to avoid all British-made clothing and to wear only American-made garments.

Soon homespun wool and linen became symbols of American virtues—hard work, thrift, and independence. In fact, the term *homespun* even became a rallying cry in the revolt against all things British. Members of the Harvard College class of 1768 wore only homespun at their graduation ceremony in Massachusetts. The *Virginia Gazette* noted that about one hundred women at a ball in Virginia in December 1769 also wore homespun. In 1770 the *Pennsylvania Gazette* reported that members of a patriotic organization called the Daughters of Liberty had dressed in homespun and gathered with their spinning wheels to rally people to resist the British.

MEN IN UNIFORM

The tensions between the American colonies and Great Britain eventually led to the Revolutionary War, a war for American independence. During the war, American farmers, woodsmen, and laborers volunteered to fight the British. Compared to the well-organized British troops, splendidly dressed in matching red-coated uniforms, the colonial army was a ragtag bunch. At the start of the war, the men wore no regular uniforms. American general George Washington recommended that they simply wear their hunting and work clothes:

- **breeches**
- **buckskin (deerskin) tunics**
- **linen shirts**
- **vests**
- **tricornes** (three-cornered-hats)

These American soldiers dress in the official uniform of the Continental Army during the Revolutionary War: blue coats, vests, buckskin breeches, boots, and tricornes.

MACARONIS IN AMERICA

In 1772 some rich young Englishmen created what they called the Macaroni Club. The men had toured Italy and had returned home to London sporting new fashions. These included tight breeches and huge wigs worn with small hats. While other men wore long jackets, members of the Macaroni Club modeled short, form-fitting jackets. They tucked big bunches of flowers into their jacket lapels. Fancy ruffles peeked from beneath their jacket sleeves. Their stockings were decorated with spots. Their shoes had tassels. They carried swords dangling from long straps.

Soon Macaroni style reached America. One of the richest men in prerevolutionary America, Bostonian shipper John Hancock (a signer of the Declaration of Independence), was a Macaroni. The militia, or citizen army, of the Maryland colony wore fancy Macaroni-style uniforms.

During the Revolutionary War, a British doctor named Richard Shuckburgh saw some sloppy colonial soldiers from Connecticut. He joked that the grubby troops thought that a lone feather in their caps made them look fashionable. He went on to write the following verse: "Yankee Doodle went to town / A-Riding on a pony / He stuck a feather in his cap / And called it macaroni."

At first British soldiers sang the song to tease their American adversaries. But after an American victory at Lexington and Concord, Massachusetts, in 1775, colonists sang the song themselves with pride. In 1978 "Yankee Doodle" became the state song of Connecticut.

In 1779 the Second Continental Congress, acting as a temporary government for the colonies, established an official American uniform. The outfit, for both enlisted men and officers, consisted of a tricorne; a vest; buckskin breeches; and a blue coat with a white, red, or tan facing (strips of buttons down the front), depending on the regiment. Men wore shoulder patches and badges on their hats to signify their military rank. Some officers wore colored ribbons across their chests.

The colonies didn't have much money and therefore couldn't afford to completely clothe every soldier. Many men didn't get the full uniform. Some had to go without shoes or coats. When soldiers' uniforms ripped or wore out, the army did not always replace them.

Women couldn't join the colonial army, but colonial women still helped the war effort. Esther de Berdt Reed, the wife of

The Ladies of Philadelphia sew shirts for General Washington's army in 1780. This group of women formed in 1778 to help provide U.S. soldiers with the clothes they needed for military wear.

Pennsylvania's governor, started a group called the Ladies of Philadelphia in 1778. Reed and other women walked door to door, collecting donations from more than sixteen hundred people. They raised $7,000 for the American troops. On General Washington's suggestion, the women used the money to buy linen and began sewing shirts for soldiers. The Ladies of Philadelphia ended up making twenty-two hundred shirts. Each woman sewed her name in the shirts she made.

Meanwhile, Americans continued to boycott British-made cloth and clothing. During the war, women dressed in

- **HOMESPUN SKIRTS**
- *jackets*
- **APRONS**
- CAPS

DID SHE OR DIDN'T SHE?
BETSY ROSS AND THE STARS AND STRIPES

Most schoolchildren learn that Betsy Ross (1752–1836) sewed the first American flag, but historians aren't sure if the story is true. What they do know is that Elizabeth (Betsy) Ross was a trained upholsterer during the Revolutionary War. At her shop in Philadelphia, she sewed and mended curtains, bedspreads, tablecloths, rugs, and other cloth goods.

The Birth of the Flag, a painting by Henry Mosler (1841–1920), shows Betsy Ross and her assistants sewing the Stars and Stripes. Historians aren't sure whether Ross really made the first flag.

She had opened the business with her first husband, John Ross. When he died during an accidental explosion, she ran the shop on her own. She also made and mended uniforms, tents, blankets, and flags for the Continental Army.

According to oral history, or stories passed down through the generations, George Washington and two other men visited Ross in 1777. Washington carried a piece of paper with a design for a flag. The sketch showed thirteen six-pointed stars and thirteen red and white stripes. The thirteen stars and stripes stood for the thirteen British colonies of North America. The story says that Ross changed Washington's design. She suggested that the thirteen stars should have five points instead of six. Then she created the first flag, called the Stars and Stripes.

Historians have found no written evidence to support this story, but Betsy Ross has nevertheless gone down in history as the woman who sewed the Stars and Stripes. The Continental Congress adopted it as the national American flag on June 14, 1777.

Chapter Two

FASHIONABLE LADIES

This 1780s woman achieves an hourglass shape by wearing a corset under her gown.

While most Revolutionary-era American women wore simple homemade clothes, wealthy women wore the latest styles from Europe. They and their families often traveled by boat across the Atlantic Ocean, bringing back fine fabrics, hats, ribbons, shoes, and other stylish accessories from European capitals. Margaret Manigault, wife of a well-to-do Virginia architect, wrote to a friend living in Paris, France, "Our modes [styles] change almost as rapidly here as they do with you."

During the war, wealthy women continued to wear the basic gown worn in colonial days. Skirts were long and full, often made of a rich, textured silk called brocade. They were split in front to reveal a petticoat—frequently embroidered with flowers and other designs. Bodices (the upper portions of dresses) were tight. Women achieved an hourglass shape—wide at the bust and hips and narrow at the waist—by wearing corsets beneath their dresses. These undergarments were lined with whalebone—stiff material from the jaws of whales—and laced snugly around the wearer's midsection.

Soon after the war, softer and less formal dresses replaced the stiff, colonial-era brocade gowns. The new styles were made of silk or printed cotton. They had floor-length full skirts with a wide sash tied around the waist. Necklines were low cut, and women filled them in with large, gauzy scarves. This fashion was called the pouter-pigeon look because the scarves puffed out in front like a pigeon's large, curved breast.

These clothes were complicated to make. The bodices had to be fitted exactly to the wearer. Wealthy women hired skilled dressmakers to fit and stitch gowns by hand. A woman and her dressmaker consulted with each other to choose fabrics and styles, as well as lace, ribbons, and other trimmings.

ALMOST NAKED!

In the 1790s, shortly after the Revolution, a shocking new woman's dress came to the United States from France. Inspired by styles of the ancient world, the new dress mimicked the clinging draped garments seen on ancient Greek and Roman statues. The French called the style *à l'antique* (like the ancients). It was later called the Empire style. The new style was a narrow one-piece dress with a high waist positioned just under the breasts. The dress also had a daringly low neckline and very short puffed sleeves that bared the arms.

Unlike full-skirted gowns in heavy fabrics that hid women's bodies, Empire-style dresses were made of thin cotton muslin—a plain, finely woven fabric—usually white. The fabric clung to wearers' legs and showed off their figures. (The style

In this 1794 oil painting, Margaret Manigault wears gauzy scarves at her neckline. Society women such as Manigault followed the latest fashions from Europe.

This cartoon from 1810 titled *The Graces in a High Wind, a Scene Taken from Nature in Kensington Gardens* pokes fun at dresses that clung too closely to women's bodies.

looked best on slender young women.) Sometimes, in a rain shower, the dresses clung too much. Cartoons of the day poked fun, showing women with dresses caught in their buttocks in back or plastered to their bodies. Because the dresses hung straight down from a high waistline, eliminating the hourglass figure, some daring women even left off their corsets.

When Americans first saw the style, many were shocked. In 1800 Abigail Adams, the wife of U.S. president John Adams, saw visiting Frenchwomen wearing Empire-style dresses at social gatherings in Philadelphia, Pennsylvania. In a letter, she expressed her disapproval:

The stile of dress . . . is really an outrage upon all decency. I will describe it as it has appeard even at the drawing Room [formal receptions] . . . a Muslin sometimes, sometimes a crape [crepe] made so strait before as perfectly to show the whole form. The arm naked almost to the shoulder and without stays [corset] or Bodice . . . and the "rich

Luxurience of natures Charms" [the breasts] without a hankerchief fully displayed.

One young woman in Baltimore, Maryland, wore a French-made dress so daring that a Mrs. Smith, a U.S. society lady, wrote in a letter, "Mobs of boys have crowded round her . . . to see what I hope will not often be seen in this country, an almost naked woman."

Although such extremes were not common, the white muslin chemise, as the Empire-style dress was also called, eventually caught on in the United States. Women loved its soft, girlish look. And they loved going without layers of full, heavy petticoats. However, most women didn't feel comfortable without a little something underneath, so they usually wore a lightweight corset and a narrow petticoat.

American Margaret Siddons Kintzing wears a chemise, also known as an Empire-style dress, in 1812. The style was considered risqué at the time because it showed more of the wearer's shape and flesh than earlier styles.

" MRS. BONAPARTE [A FRENCH ARISTOCRAT] CAME TO A DANCE GIVEN BY MRS. SMITH (IN WASHINGTON) WEARING A DRESS SO TRANSPARENT THAT YOU COULD SEE THE COLOR AND SHAPE OF HER THIGHS, AND EVEN MORE! "

—ROSALIE STIER CALVERT, WIFE OF A WEALTHY MARYLAND PLANTATION OWNER, 1804

TONING IT DOWN: *The Jane Austen Era*

Over time the Empire style changed to become more practical and wearable. Dressmakers added longer sleeves. In 1814 British author Jane Austen wrote in a letter, "I wear my gauze [muslin] gown today long sleeves & all. . . . Mrs. Tilson. . . has assured me that they are worn in the evening by many." Women filled in low necklines with a handkerchief or a tucker (also called a chemisette). This cloth, usually white, had high ruffles around the neck and tucked into the dress at the neckline. One portrait from the early 1800s of style setter Dolley Madison, wife of former U.S. president James Madison, shows her wearing a tucker.

Chemises were no good in cold weather or in the chilly, poorly heated houses of the time. Some wealthy women became ill with flu while wearing the flimsy dresses. People even called influenza the muslin disease. For extra warmth, some women covered chemises with short, fitted jackets called spencers—made of wool, silk, or velvet. Others donned pelisses, or high-waisted coat dresses.

Instead of muslin, some chemises were made of percale, a slightly heavier cotton. Others were made of calico—a printed, checked, or striped cotton. For formal chemises, dressmakers used silk. They embellished the original simple shape with ruffles, lace, and garlands of flowers.

First Lady Dolley Madison wears a white ruffled collar with her dress in this 1817 portrait. Madison was the wife of President James Madison and was admired for her style.

THE *Victorian* IDEAL

The years 1820 to 1860 are called the early Victorian era in both the United States and Great Britain. This name comes from the long reign (1837–1901) of Britain's beloved Queen Victoria.

The fashions of this era expressed the image of the Victorian woman, who was expected to be modest and pure, or the "angel in the house." This term was inspired by a popular poem of that name written by British author Coventry Patmore about his wife. Society expected Victorian women to be devoted, self-sacrificing wives and mothers and to uphold high moral values. Louisa May Alcott's novel *Little Women* (1868 and 1869) describes the fictional March sisters, growing up in New England in the mid–1800s. Marmee, the girls' mother, sums up Victorian attitudes this way:

> I want my daughters to be beautiful, accomplished, and good . . . to be well and wisely married, and to lead useful, pleasant lives. . . . To be loved and chosen by a good man is the best and sweetest thing which can happen to a woman . . . when the happy time comes, [I hope] you may feel ready for the duties and worthy of the joy.

Middle-class women like the March girls were expected to be all this, plus do the housework. But a well-to-do Victorian wife was an "ornament" in her husband's home.

The Victorian era was named for Britain's Queen Victoria, shown here in this painting from 1842. The era was marked by strict rules about dress and behavior, especially for women.

She was a "lady" who didn't do any heavy work—that was left to the servants. Instead, she learned proper manners, hosted social gatherings, and did needlework and other light domestic arts.

PLUMP AND PECULIAR

Around 1830 a new look emerged on the U.S. fashion scene. Above triangular skirts, the dress featured huge leg-of-mutton sleeves—so called because they resembled fat legs of lamb. The sleeves were so wide that they required sleeve plumpers, pads that tied at the shoulders underneath the dress. The pads filled out the sleeves so they wouldn't droop.

An illustration from an 1833 issue of *Godey's Lady's Book* shows a dress with leg-of-mutton sleeves.

PRIM *and Proper*

When the Victorian ideal of womanhood took hold, the light, unrestricted Empire-style gown went out of fashion. Dress waistlines went downward, tight corsets returned, and skirts got fuller. The emphasis shifted from the bosom to the waist.

Well-off Victorian women were cinched in and weighed down. To achieve the tiniest waist possible, women wore tightly laced, heavily boned corsets. Floor-length skirts could be as wide as 10 yards (9 meters) around the hem. Along with the five or six petticoats needed to make a skirt stand out, these clothes were heavy, hot, and restrictive.

The Victorian idea of dress was the more the better. Fabric patterns ran from flower-sprigged prints to bold plaids, checks, and stripes. Many dresses were elaborately decorated with

- LACE
- *Trims*
- RUFFLES
- PLEATS
- SCALLOPS
- FLOUNCES
- *Fringe*

For formal parties, balls, and dinners, dresses were low cut. A low, wide collar called a bertha showed off a woman's shoulders and neck. She usually added decorations such as artificial flowers, ribbons, jeweled pins, and feathers to her hair.

WHAT THE GIRLS WORE

Until the late 1700s, European and American parents thought of and treated children as miniature adults. Girls dressed like their mothers and even began wearing training corsets as young as the age of four.

But French philosopher Jean-Jacques Rousseau put forth new ideas in the mid-1700s. He said that children should not be forced to grow up too soon and that they should be free to run and play. In response to Rousseau, Europeans and Americans stopped dressing children like adults. Little girls' clothes became looser and simpler.

In the United States, girls started wearing soft cotton chemises, with scooped necks and short sleeves. When the chemise style went out of fashion, girls once again wore dresses with snug bodices and full skirts. But a girl's skirts were shorter than her mother's—reaching to about mid-calf—so she had more freedom of movement.

Beneath their skirts, young girls wore pantalets. These loose, ruffled, cotton pants reached below the knee and showed beneath a girl's skirts. To keep her clothes clean, a girl wore an apron or a pinafore—a loose sleeveless cotton cover-up.

Once a girl became a teenager, however, she dressed like her mother. She stopped wearing pantalets and pinafores. She put on a boned corset and wore her skirts long.

U.S. artist John F. Francis painted this picture of his daughter Mary in the 1840s. She wears a loose dress with cotton pantalets underneath.

Artist John Singleton Copley created this oil painting of Henry Laurens in 1782. Laurens is wearing a frock coat over a waistcoat, a white linen shirt, knee breeches, stockings, and buckled shoes. Laurens was president of the Continental Congress (the U.S. government during the Revolution) in 1777 and 1778.

Chapter Three

FINE GENTLEMEN

Like their wives, wealthy Revolutionary-era men dressed in styles worn by the French nobility. The wealthy man's basic ensemble was rich and ornate, especially for formal occasions. He wore a full-skirted frock coat of satin, silk, or wool over a richly embroidered waistcoat (like a long vest). Under that was a finely made white linen shirt. Knee breeches, worn with silk stockings and buckled shoes, completed the outfit. Some frock coats sported elegant military-style gold braid and metal buttons.

A wealthy man always wore a wig—made of human hair or cheaper hair from a horse or a goat. Wigs were styled with a roll or two of curls over the ears and a queue—a tail hanging down the back. Men dusted their wigs with white or gray powder. They cut their own hair very short or even shaved it all off so that their wigs fit better. A bald head probably also made wearing a wig more comfortable, since heavy wigs could be hot and itchy inside.

A NEW SUIT

During the French Revolution (1789–1799), the people of France overthrew their king and set up a new government. Afterward, both American and European men rejected elaborate French styles. Just as American women began wearing simpler, less formal clothes, so did men.

Wealthy American men picked up a dashing new style worn by the British gentry. Originally for horseback riding, the new look featured tall leather boots, polished to a high shine and worn with pantaloons—tight, smooth-fitting knee-length breeches. The most fashionable pantaloons were made of soft buckskin, sometimes soaked in water so they would shrink and dry to a skintight fit.

A well-fitted tailcoat (a waist-length garment with long tails in back) replaced the old colonial frock coat. Instead of the colorful satins and silks of colonial coats, tailcoats were made of fine dark wool, in browns, blues, and greens. A short vest was worn underneath.

A white shirt worn under the vest and coat was the hallmark of a wealthy and well-dressed man. At the neck, the elegant man wore a cravat, or neck cloth. This long band of white muslin could be wrapped and tied in a dozen or more ways. The best-dressed men were experts at tying their cravats (either by themselves or with the help of a valet, or servant). The intricate wrapping and knot-tying styles had such names as

- **the Oriental**
- **the Mathematical**
- **the American**

Some men wrapped multiple cravats high

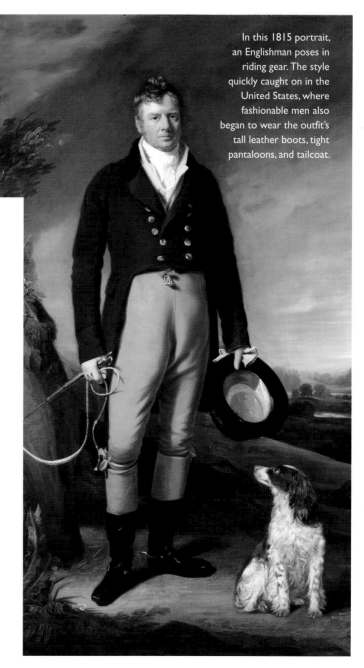

In this 1815 portrait, an Englishman poses in riding gear. The style quickly caught on in the United States, where fashionable men also began to wear the outfit's tall leather boots, tight pantaloons, and tailcoat.

around their necks, until they could barely bend their heads. A young woman named Juliana Gales Seaton wrote in 1812 that her brother and a friend "started in fine style, the latter sporting *five* cravats, Joseph contenting himself with *three*."

THE FIRST BATHROBES

If a wealthy man in Revolutionary-era America wanted to relax at home without his coat, he put on a loose garment called a banyan over his shirt and breeches. Made of printed silk imported from India by way of Britain, this garment was a little like a modern bathrobe. Around the house, a man might also exchange his itchy wig for a soft dome-shaped cap—also of Indian origin.

In this illustration from 1812, a man wears five short capes over his greatcoat.

Nicolas Boylston (1747–1828), a wealthy Boston merchant, wears a banyan over his shirt in this oil painting by John Singleton Copley.

For riding horses, walking, or travel, a wealthy man wore a greatcoat. This long woolen coat had buttons down the front and one or more short capes attached to the shoulders. Multiple capes were all the fashion. In extreme cases, a man might wear a dozen.

Gradually, men's coats got shorter and boxier, until they looked more like the suit jackets of modern times. Trousers began to lengthen. By the early 1800s, they were ankle length. Most American men took to these new long pants right away. A British visitor to New York in 1817 noted that long "trowsers were universal." However, a few older men clung to traditional colonial styles. President James Monroe wore knee breeches and a frock coat during his term in office, from 1817 to 1825.

The Dandy

A truly elegant Victorian man wore simple yet tailored clothes of the best quality. "The best dressed persons are those in whose attire nothing in particular attracts attention," wrote Henry Lunettes in *The American Gentleman's Guide to Politeness and Fashion* in 1858.

Unlike the understated gentleman, a dandy was an overdressed showoff—a wannabe. He wore coats and pantaloons that were *too* tight, in bright colors instead of quiet, tasteful shades.

These 1850s gentlemen in New York are dressed in the height of Victorian fashion.

New York's Bowery district was home to many young working-class dandies, nicknamed b'hoys. U.S. writer Cornelius Mathews described one such young man dressed in "stark staring blue for coat, brick-red for waistcoat, breeches with a portentous [pompous] green stripe, hat brushed to the highest gloss, shiny as a new kettle."

DETACHABLE AND REPLACEABLE

Shirt collars replaced elaborate neck cloths in the early 1800s. In the 1820s, a U.S. housewife named Hannah Montague invented the detachable shirt collar *(right)*. This handy item, which was followed by detachable cuffs, buttoned onto a shirt. An old, dirty collar could be replaced with a fresh one without washing the whole shirt. Since a man's coat and vest covered up all but his collar and cuffs, those were the only parts of a shirt that needed to look clean. With a fresh collar and cuffs, a man could wear a dirty shirt without anyone noticing. The invention saved women from doing loads of laundry, which they had to do by hand in this era.

WHAT THE BOYS WORE

In the 1700s and 1800s, well-to-do mothers dressed their baby boys exactly like little girls, in simple chemise dresses with scooped necks and short sleeves. In portraits and photographs of babies and toddlers, it's impossible to tell the boys from the girls. The only clue: a girl's hair was usually parted in the middle, while boys had side parts.

In general, a boy was breeched—given his first pair of pants—between the ages of four and ten. The boy got knee breeches at first and switched to longer pants as he grew older. Breeching was an important event in a boy's life. "Going into Breeches," a poem written in 1809 by British writers Mary and Charles Lamb, celebrates the transition this way:

Joy to Philip, he this day
Has his long coats cast away,
And (the childish season gone)
Puts the manly breeches on.

Once breeched, a boy wore clothes that were miniature versions of Dad's.

Thomas "Tad" Lincoln, the youngest son of President Abraham Lincoln, is shown wearing longer pants in this 1862 photograph. As boys grew older, they made the transition from knee breeches to longer pants.

Martha Washington, the wife of President George Washington, knits in her home at Mount Vernon, Virginia, in this woodcut from the mid to late 1700s. Many clothes during this time were homemade.

Chapter Four
WHO MADE THE CLOTHES?

In Revolutionary years, all clothing in the United States was either custom made or homemade. The wealthy hired skilled tailors and dressmakers to fashion and fit their clothing to order. In some cases, wealthy women sewed their husband's white linen shirts at home, although many men had shirts custom made.

Poor and middle-class women stitched clothing for their entire families, including dresses, shirts, undergarments, and trousers. Many women also made the cloth itself. They spun wool into yarn, and cotton and flax into thread.

All women of this era started sewing as little girls. As *The Ladies' Self Instructor in Millinery and Mantua Making, Embroidery and Applique* stated, "Most girls begin dress-making very early; that is to say, when they clothe their dolls: and very good practice it is. . . . From making your doll's frocks [dresses], your next step was . . . to make your own." Students at New York's Female Academy, a school for young women, were told that needlework was "the fitting occupation of Women."

THE

LADIES' SELF INSTRUCTOR

IN

MILLINERY AND MANTUA MAKING,

EMBROIDERY AND APPLIQUE,

CANVAS-WORK, KNITTING, NETTING
AND CROCHET-WORK.

ILLUSTRATED WITH NUMEROUS ENGRAVINGS

PHILADELPHIA:
PUBLISHED BY J. & J. L. GIHON.
NO. 98 CHESNUT STREET.
1853.

The title of this 1853 book refers to "millinery and mantua making," a fancy way of saying hat and dressmaking.

Men's shirts were simple to make but required long hours of hand stitching. This tedious work—undertaken by women of all classes—inspired a poem, "The Song of the Shirt" by British humorist and poet Thomas Hood (1778–1845):

> O men with sisters dear!
> O men with mothers and wives!
> It is not the linen you're wearing out,
> But human creatures' lives.

THE CLOTH
FOR THE CLOTHES

For the upper classes, homespun and other homemade fabrics weren't good enough. Throughout the 1700s, wealthy Americans purchased high-quality cloth from abroad. Fine materials such as silk, brocade, filmy white muslin, and printed cotton came from faraway places like India and China. Good wool and cotton were made by machine in Great Britain.

In 1790 in Pawtucket, Rhode Island, Samuel Slater opened the first American cotton mill. There, workers wove cotton thread into fabric. They used mechanical looms, powered by waterwheels. Three years later, American Eli Whitney invented the cotton gin. This machine removed cottonseeds from cotton fibers much faster than could be done by hand. This enabled manufacturers to produce cotton fabric quickly and in large amounts.

In 1814 Francis Cabot Lowell of Massachusetts opened the first U.S. factory to process cotton from start to finish—from raw fibers to finished cloth. After that, the U.S. cotton industry took off. Soon cotton fabric was cheap and readily available, even in rural areas.

Eli Whitney's cotton gin, invented in 1793, revolutionized the textile industry. The machine—which cleaned cotton fiber quickly—allowed manufacturers to make large amounts of cotton cloth quickly and efficiently.

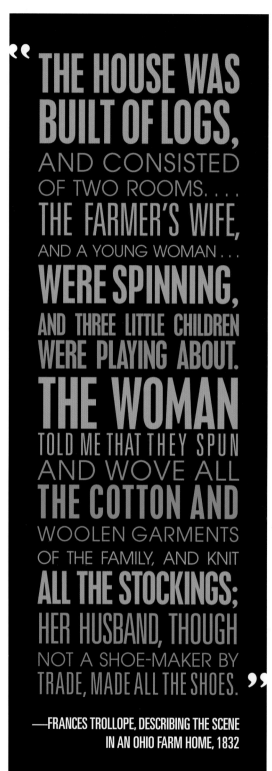

In her children's book *Little House in the Big Woods* (1932), Laura Ingalls Wilder described the many cotton fabrics for sale in a frontier store in the mid-1800s:

> The storekeeper took down bolts and bolts of beautiful calicos and spread them out.... Every new color and pattern was prettier than the last.... Ma chose two patterns of calico to make shirts for Pa, and a piece of brown denim to make him a jumper [overalls]. Then she got some white cloth to make sheets and underwear. Pa got enough calico to make Ma a new apron.... Ma smiled and flushed pink, and she picked out a pattern of rosebuds and leaves on a soft, faun-colored ground.

These women work at a textile mill in Massachusetts in the mid-1800s. They hold some of the tools used to make raw cotton into finished cloth. Mill workers provided the fabric from which ready-to-wear clothing was made.

Tailor-Made
OR READY-MADE?

Throughout the 1700s, tailors and dressmakers made clothing to order. That is, they took a customer's measurements and stitched garments specifically tailored for that person. Custom-made clothing was expensive. Only the wealthy could afford it. Everyone else wore homemade clothing.

The situation changed in the early 1800s, when tailors began to make ready-made clothing for men. Ready-made clothing was not tailored for one specific customer. Instead, tailors made coats and jackets in standard sizes—small, medium, and large. Customers could try on ready-made clothing to find the size that fit. Because it didn't require precise personal measurements and fittings, ready-made clothing was much more affordable than custom-made clothing.

Shopping emporiums specializing in ready-made men's clothing soon opened in big cities. In New York, John Williams opened his elegant Gentlemen's Fashionable Wearing Apparel Warehouse in 1816. In 1818 Henry Sands Brooks opened another New York clothing store, which later became Brooks Brothers. Also in New York, Samuel Whitmarsh's shop on Broadway sold complete men's suits. The store also sold these:

- **cravats**
- **handkerchiefs**
- **stockings**
- **suspenders**
- **collars**

MADE IN AMERICA

Hat making was one of the first successful industries in America. The first American hat factory opened in Danbury, Connecticut, in 1780. By 1800 Danbury was the nation's hat-making center. For a time, it was the hat capital of the world. Men's hats of this era, in both Europe and the United States, were usually of felted (matted) wool or beaver fur. The fur to make the hats also came from America. In the 1780s, American fur traders sold about thirty thousand beaver pelts each year to European hat merchants.

Brooks Clothing Store, seen in this 1864 illustration of the store in New York, sold men's fashions. This store later expanded all over the United States with the name Brooks Brothers.

City streets soon began to bustle with shoppers. One observer described the New York scene: "The carmen [carriage drivers] halloo [shout] and lash their horses . . . well-dressed men of all ages . . . and fashion of apparel and manner, throng the way . . . the whole scene is . . . dazzling, and delightful."

THE MIDDLE CLASS GETS DRESSED

After the Revolutionary War, the American middle class grew quickly. More people began to settle in towns and in growing cities. People in a wide variety of professions—doctors, lawyers, and shopkeepers—made up the new middle class. These workers were all men. Their wives didn't work outside the home.

The new U.S. middle class took pride in wearing pretty much the same clothing styles that wealthy people wore. They didn't have enough money to buy the finest silks and laces, but they wanted to look good. For men, the ready-made clothing industry made that possible. In city shops, middle-class men could buy ready-made coats, shirts, and trousers in fashionable styles and at reasonable prices. In the 1840s, one European observer noted that in U.S. cities, even store clerks were "dressed in a way we [in Europe] are accustomed to see only among the gentry."

For women, ready-made skirts and dresses weren't available until later in the 1800s. For most of the century, women had to sew their own clothing at home or hire a dressmaker if they could afford it. But women could buy ready-made accessories, such as caps, aprons, and corsets. And even without ready-made outfits, middle-class women could usually dress well. They could buy U.S.-made cottons and other fabrics. They could even hire a dressmaker once or twice a year to help them measure, cut out, and hand stitch clothing for themselves and their families. Many could afford one silk dress for visiting and another, fancier one for parties and dinners.

Edwin Stanton (1814–1869), a lawyer and later secretary of war under President Abraham Lincoln, wears a three-piece suit in this photograph from the mid-1800s. A wealthier man of this era would have worn a very similar suit, though made from a more expensive fabric.

THE QUEEN OF INVENTIONS

Until 1845 all clothing—even the ready-made variety—was sewn by hand, stitch by stitch. All that changed with the sewing machine, invented by Massachusetts-born Elias Howe. A few years after Howe, U.S. inventor Isaac Singer created a more efficient sewing machine.

With a sewing machine, long seams that took hours to sew by hand could be stitched up in minutes. The women's magazine *Godey's Lady's Book* called the sewing machine the Queen of Inventions. *Godey's* reported that "a gentleman's shirt required one hour and sixteen minutes by machine and fourteen hours and twenty-six minutes by hand."

The sewing machine revolutionized the ready-made clothing industry. With sewing machines, manufacturers turned out garments more quickly and in greater volume than ever before. Because they required less time and labor, garments were less expensive to buy.

In addition to machines for manufacturers, Singer's company created sewing machines for home use. For women who could afford them, sewing machines cut hours from the time needed to make a family's clothing.

With sewing machines, manufacturers could churn out thousands of affordable, ready-made garments. This machine was invented by Elias Howe in 1846.

This illustration from the 1830s shows a variety of women's accessories: handkerchiefs, gloves, bonnets, and other adornments.

Chapter Five

HIDDEN AND
FOR SHOW

Men and women of the 1700s and 1800s were weighed down with loads of extras every time they got dressed. Women wore complicated layers of undergarments. In addition, hats, gloves, handkerchiefs, and other accessories for both sexes made getting ready for a dinner with friends or an afternoon visit a complicated operation.

WOMEN'S BODY SHAPERS

With their small waists and full skirts, women's clothes required a shapely framework underneath. To achieve it, stylish women wore layers and layers of fussy petticoats, along with tight, waist-pinching corsets—winter and summer.

Originally called stays, corsets were boned. They contained narrow vertical channels, into which corset makers inserted thin whalebones. With the help of a servant or a family member, a woman laced her corset tightly. The garments laced at either the back or the front—sometimes both. The effect was to cinch in the woman's waist and push up her breasts. This shaped her upper body properly for her dresses. Wearing a corset did enforce good posture. However, the tighter the corset was laced, the harder it was for a woman to be active or even to take a deep breath.

Whether a woman was a servant or the wife of a wealthy man, a corset was a must. For any woman to go without one would have been improper. However, women working on farms and around the house didn't lace their corsets tightly. They needed freedom of movement. And when loosely laced, a corset actually helped support a woman's back during long days of bending and lifting.

Women wore layers of petticoats under their dresses to make their skirts fuller. This 1852 illustration in the *World of Fashion* shows a woman lifting her skirt to reveal a petticoat.

Stylish women, though, wore their corsets as tight as they could stand them. In *Little Women*, modest Meg allows her fashionable friends to dress her in unaccustomed high style for a party. As author Louisa May Alcott described it, "They laced her into a sky-blue dress, which was so tight she could hardly breathe."

WHALES AND WARDROBES

The whalebones used in corsets *(right)* weren't actually the bones of whales. They were made of baleen. Baleen are comblike plates in the jaws of certain whales. Whales use baleen to filter fish and other food from the large mouthfuls of water they take in.

Baleen is a tough natural substance—the same material that makes up claws or fingernails. Sometimes described as the plastic of the 1700s and 1800s, baleen is strong yet light and flexible. Clothing makers used it in all sorts of garments and accessories. They split it into slender pieces for corset stays and hoopskirts. They used it to make the ribs of parasols (umbrellas) and to stiffen men's shirt collars.

The tighter the corset, the higher a woman's wealth and social standing. The message was that a well-to-do woman can afford to be idle. She has servants to do her work for her (and to tie up her corset laces). Also, the ideal Victorian woman was supposed to be appealingly weak and helpless—dependent on her husband to protect and care for her. Yet middle-class women, who had to do most of their own housework, followed the tight-lacing fashion as faithfully as the wealthy. The look said clearly: "I'm a lady too."

WOMEN'S UNDERWEAR
Easy-Breezy

The innermost layer of a woman's underwear was a shift (also called a chemise)—a loose, one-piece linen garment, knee-length, with short sleeves. Underpants, called drawers, weren't added until the 1840s. Made of linen, cotton, or wool, with a drawstring waist, drawers looked like baggy knee-length shorts. But unlike shorts, drawers had no seam at the crotch. This made it easier to use the bathroom since tight corsets and layers of petticoats were hard to manage.

Full skirts required layers of petticoats to shape them. The petticoats of the late 1700s included a fancy embroidered or quilted satin petticoat worn for show. This outermost petticoat showed under the split-front skirt of a gown. Beneath this, women wore plainer white linen or cotton under-petticoats. Heavy wool petticoats kept women warm in winter.

With the narrow, high-waisted Empire style, women wore fewer petticoats. Some women didn't wear any. But as wide gathered skirts came back into fashion in the early 1800s, women wore more and more layers of petticoats—four to six layers that could weigh up to 30 pounds (14 kilograms).

Around 1856 the cage crinoline appeared. This new invention lightened the load by eliminating the need for multiple petticoats. A cage crinoline consisted of a series of nine to eighteen steel hoops. Each hoop was wider than the one above. They were connected to one another by strong cloth tapes. This contraption supported very wide skirts yet weighed very little.

This photo from the 1850s shows a cage crinoline. The woman will cover the cage with one or more skirts.

"SPENT ALL AFTERNOON IN SEWING ROOM WITH MAMA. . . RIPPED LACE OFF OLD BLUE SATIN EVENING GOWN. . . INSERTED TWO NEW WHALEBONES IN CORSET AS OLD ONES WERE BENT AND UNCOMFORTABLE. . . SEWED NEW TAPES IN HOOP. . . RAN FRESH RIBBONS IN CHEMISES & CORSET COVERS."

—YOUNG WOMAN'S JOURNAL ENTRY, MID-1800S

In her memoir of life in the late 1800s, British writer Gwen Raverat recalled, "Once I asked Aunt Etty what it had been like to wear a crinoline. 'Oh, it was delightful' she said. 'I've never been so comfortable. . . . It kept your petticoats away from your legs, and made walking so light and easy.'"

Cage crinolines led to plenty of humor. A British cartoon of the time, called "A Windy Day," showed a woman with hoopskirts blown up over her head. American newspapers published exaggerated reports of women unable to fit into carriages or through doorways and of sweeping skirts knocking over furniture and ornaments in drawing rooms. Reporters also wrote about skirts going up in flames when they got too close to the fireplace. Some of these stories were true. Women did have to be careful near fire, which could turn their skirts into blazing infernos.

Despite the laughter, cage crinolines became very popular. In the United States, an estimated 3,000 tons (2,721 metric tons) of steel were used to manufacture them. In reality, the very wide, exaggerated versions were reserved for magazine illustrations and fancy formal occasions. For everyday wear, most women wore smaller hoops.

Hair and Hats

Before and during the Revolutionary era, fashionable women sported big, elaborate hairdos. With the help of a maid or a professional hairdresser, they styled their hair into tight, frizzy curls. They combed the curls over pads of wool or horsehair, placed close to the scalp. Only women who were wealthy enough to have servants or hairdressers could wear this time-consuming style.

This British cartoon pokes fun at cage crinolines. The woman in this 1860s illustration can't fit through the door of a carriage. Some American women encountered the same problem.

Esther Boardman, the sister of a U.S. senator, sports a popular hairdo of the time—with curls falling down her neck and a feather in her hair— in this 1789 painting by Ralph Earl.

- **kill beaus**
- **heartbreakers**
- **beau catchers**

As these names imply, women believed that prettily styled hairpieces would help them attract male suitors. On a visit to the United States, Frances Trollope sarcastically noted of American women: "They are . . . most unhappily partial to false hair, which they wear in surprising quantities . . . it is less trouble to append [attach] a bunch of waving curls here, there, and every where, than to keep their native tresses [their own hair] in perfect order."

After the Revolution, women stopped wearing padded hairdos. They wore their long hair parted it in the middle. They arranged it in curls or braids, which were pulled up on top of the head or left to cascade down the back of the neck. One pretty hairdo featured a mass of curls or a twisted knot on top of the head. Rosalie Stier Calvert, wife of a wealthy Maryland plantation owner, wrote in an 1804 letter to her mother in Europe, "I am including here a small drawing showing how we do our hair . . . sometimes with a garland of flowers, or the hair is turned up with combs garnished [adorned] with pearls, or for those who have them, diamonds."

For extra fullness, some women wore hairpieces, called by colorful names like these:

In this illustration from 1832, a woman stands at her dressing table, looking in a mirror. Hairpieces hang from the edge of the table.

No woman in Revolutionary or early Victorian times—rich or poor—would have been caught dead without a hat when she went out. Even at home, women wore a soft cap of white linen or muslin, sometimes tied with ribbons under the chin. The only exception was a formal evening occasion. Then, instead of hats, wealthy women wore hair ornaments such as these:

- **feathers**
- **flowers**
- **ribbons**
- **decorative combs**

The high, wide hairstyles of the late 1700s required big hats. Frances Trollope, visiting Trenton, New Jersey, saw "pretty ladies . . . with their expansive bonnets, any one of which might handsomely have filled the space allotted to three." Wide-brimmed hats of straw, chip (a cheaper version of straw), and felted (matted) fur were popular. A high silk bonnet called a calash was specially made to protect large

Bonnets with ribbons that tied under the chin were popular for much of the 1800s. This woman wears a decorated bonnet in 1852.

This American calash from 1775 protected women's large hairdos.

hairdos. The bonnet had a stiff inner frame of cane or whalebone to hold it above the hair. The hat got its name because it was shaped like the hood of a calash, a small carriage with a folding top.

A headwear craze in the early 1800s was the turban. This type of hat was made of a long coiled silk cloth and was based on styles worn in Turkey and the Middle East. First Lady Dolley Madison was famous for wearing turbans. She appeared at her husband's inaugural ball in 1809 wearing a satin and velvet turban decorated with bird of paradise feathers.

In the 1820s, women began to wear prim bonnets with brims that framed their faces and ribbons that tied under their chins. This style stayed popular for most of the century. The bonnets were decorated with flowers, feathers, and ribbons. Women could buy bonnets from a milliner (hatmaker) or make their own. To update an old bonnet, women got creative and added new trimmings.

HANDS *and* FEET

Like hats, gloves were considered a necessary accessory for any proper woman in the revolutionary and early Victorian years. Bare hands were only for working women and slaves. A lady had to keep her hands soft. Made of soft leather or silk, gloves could be pulled up above the elbow for evening wear or pushed down near the wrists for day wear. Gloves were necessary for dancing, because in public, men and women were not supposed to touch each other with bare hands. Many working women wore mitts— fingerless gloves that kept their arms and hands warm but left their fingers free to sew and do other tasks. But mitts also became fashionable for wealthy women. They were sometimes made in lacy openwork designs.

In the 1700s, wealthy and fashionable women wore leather shoes, with thick, hourglass-shaped heels, about 2 inches (5 centimeters) tall. Some shoes had large removable metal buckles, so the wearer could use them on more than one pair of shoes. Around the beginning of the next century, dainty, flat-heeled kidskin (goatskin) or silk slippers replaced buckled shoes for wealthy women. Some slippers had crisscrossed ribbon ties. These shoes nicely complemented the new high-waisted Empire-style dresses of this era. Outdoors, some women wore half boots—low boots that buttoned up on the sides. Women often wore pattens in wet and muddy conditions. These were wooden soles attached to iron platforms. They tied onto shoes to raise the wearer above the muck.

This woman from the 1850s shows off stylish lacy mitts, or fingerless gloves.

These white satin women's shoes of the mid-1700s had hourglass-shaped heels and fancy fringe.

Fine leather and kidskin shoes were expensive, and most American women couldn't afford them. Poor and working-class women often wore ill-fitting, poorly made leather shoes, cobbled together at home. Women often worked barefoot in mild weather.

All the Extras

Until the late 1700s, women carried small necessities in pockets. Unlike modern pockets, a pocket was a hanging fabric bag with a slit opening. A woman tied the bag around her waist, under her skirts. Both skirts and petticoats had slits in the sides, so a woman could reach her hand inside, into her pocket. Women often made pockets from pretty scraps of fabric. They stitched the fabric into a patchwork design or embroidered it with fancy decorations.

Pockets were too bulky for narrow, high-waisted Empire-style dresses. When wearing these dresses, women carried reticules—the first purses. These were simple drawstring bags, often painted or embroidered. Fancy ones were knitted from silk or intricately beaded. What did a woman carry in her reticule? In 1853 *Godey's Lady's Book* advised, "As the reticule is only intended to hold a handkerchief, it need not be very large."

A silk parasol protected a woman's skin from the sun and looked charming as well. The most popular parasols in the early 1800s were green, trimmed with gold fringe. In the rain, women carried more practical umbrellas made of oiled silk.

Fans, made of paper, silk, lace, or even feathers, were attached to sticks of carved

The woman in this 1810s illustration holds a parasol in one hand and a reticule in the other. Fans like the one shown below were also common accessories.

wood, ivory, tortoiseshell, or bone. They were useful for cooling oneself in hot, stuffy drawing rooms and ballrooms. But they were also tools for flirting. A woman could hold her fan in front of her face to attract attention to her pretty eyes or to halfway hide a becoming blush. Fans were often very beautiful and elaborate. Many were intricately painted with landscapes or with floral and other motifs.

MEN'S UNDERWEAR: ALL IN ONE

A man's basic underwear consisted of just a cotton or linen shirt, cut long, to about mid-thigh. The long tails covered up his backside and tucked into his breeches or trousers all around. Actually, this shirt was both underwear and outerwear. It was the shirt worn directly beneath a waistcoat. But when covered by a waistcoat and then a frock coat, only the shirt collar and cuffs showed.

Because the shirt was also underwear, a gentleman never appeared in public without at least a waistcoat to cover it. But laboring men often worked in just a shirt and breeches, especially in hot weather. Around 1807 magazines began recommending that men wear drawers for cleanliness. Made of washable cotton or linen, these loose undergarments left the crotch seam open, as in women's drawers.

This waistcoat from the 1840s is intricately patterned.

HEAD TO FOOT

A true gentleman of the Revolutionary or early Victorian era *always* wore a hat when he went out. Both soldiers and civilian (nonmilitary) men wore tricornes. These hats had a wide brim, normally turned up in three places. Working men turned the brim down all around to keep off the sun and rain.

In the 1790s, wealthy men began wearing top hats with tall crowns and narrow brims. The hats were made of felted beaver fur or black silk. In 1823 Frenchman Antoine Gibus invented a collapsible top hat, which took up much less room on a shelf. Inside, the hat had thin steel springs, which allowed it to fold down flat. Top hats came to be associated with upper-class men and even with Uncle Sam, a symbol for the U.S. government. Drawings from the 1830s show Uncle Sam as a tall, thin man in a top hat.

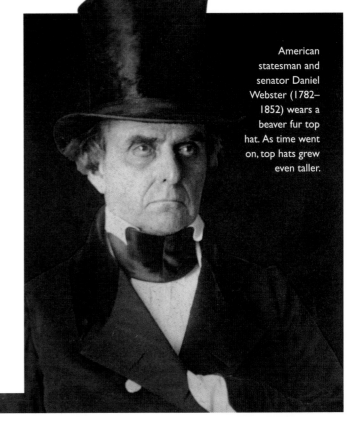

American statesman and senator Daniel Webster (1782–1852) wears a beaver fur top hat. As time went on, top hats grew even taller.

TWO LEFT FEET

Prior to the 1800s, shoemakers made shoes on a single straight last, or wooden form. So each shoe was identical in shape. There were no left and right shoes. Eventually, the shoes molded themselves to the wearer's feet. In 1800 Philadelphia boot maker William Young introduced right and left shoes, but these were not common until later in the century.

Wealthy colonial-era men wore shoes very similar to women's. They were made of black leather, with chunky 1-inch (2.5 cm) heels and buckles. Around 1800 this style gave way to flat shoes with laces, much like those that modern men wear. For riding or walking, men wore tall boots inspired by military wear.

Workingmen wore much less elegant homemade boots and shoes. Homemade footwear often fit poorly. Some men stuffed their oversized shoes with rags to improve the fit. Like women, poor men often went barefoot in summer.

In the 1820s, the ready-made shoe business began to boom. By 1835 U.S. shoemakers were producing more than fifteen million pairs of ready-made shoes each year. The prices were reasonable, and even working people could afford them.

ALL THE *Extras*

In addition to shoes and hats, men used and carried a wide assortment of accessories. A Virginia milliner named Catherine Rathell stocked many men's accessories imported from London. They included "shoe and knee buckles [for breeches], watches, Morocco leather pocketbooks . . . memorandum books, razors, pocket knives and forks, tobacco, and 'Thread hair Nets, Such as gentlemen Sleep in.'"

Wealthy men carried round pocket watches (wristwatches weren't invented until the end of the 1800s). A watch was a precious possession, passed down from father to son. A man carried his watch in a very small pocket at the top of his breeches or trousers.

This pocket watch belonged to Southern general Thomas "Stonewall" Jackson, a brilliant military commander during the Civil War (1861–1865).

Like women, wealthy men always wore leather gloves—fine ones for dress occasions and heavier ones for riding or work. For their money and important papers, men carried a leather or fabric wallet. In the 1700s, the wallet was a large, envelope-style folder carried in the hands. Wallets gradually became small enough to carry in pockets.

A walking stick was used as a fashion accessory rather than an aid in walking. Fancy ones had beautiful carved wood or metal handles. The dashing and dangerous sword cane was a wooden walking cane with a sword blade concealed inside.

HAIRY HEADS AND FACES

After the Revolutionary War, American men stopped wearing powdered wigs. Instead, men in the young United States wore their own natural hair, cut in a loose, slightly disheveled crop. Hairstyles had ancient Roman names, such as the Titus and the Brutus.

In the late 1700s and the early 1800s, whether they were rich or poor, men were always clean shaven. But around the 1820s,

A CLOSE SHAVE

Revolutionary-era barbershops weren't just places to get your hair cut. Barbers also styled wigs, shaved faces, and pulled teeth. During this era, illness was wrongly attributed to bad blood, and barbers performed bloodletting. That is, they tried to restore customers' health by making a small cut in an arm to drain out what they believed to be tainted blood.

For shaving, a barber used a straight razor, an extremely sharp blade on the end of a long handle. He lathered the customer's face and neck with soap and deftly shaved him clean. This work took skill and a steady hand—plus a lot of trust on the part of the customer.

sideburns became popular. Some men grew bushy side whiskers, called muttonchops because they looked like a couple of lamb chops stuck to a man's cheeks. Men started to sport mustaches too, either with a downward turn at the ends or with the ends curled up. The trends in facial hair began among young men in cities and then spread to other areas of the country.

Beards, however, were rare and even frowned upon. People thought they were dirty, ugly, and vulgar. In Fitchburg, Massachusetts, in 1830, one man dared to arrive at church with a beard. The minister refused him Holy Communion, a Christian ritual. Afterward, a group of townsmen attacked the bearded man with soap and razors and tried to give him a shave. By the 1850s, however, people's thinking had changed. Beards were widely accepted.

In the 1840s, men began using a product called Macassar oil to style their hair in a wave above the forehead. The messy oil even gave its name to a special kind of doily—the antimacassar. Homeowners placed antimacassars on the backs of chairs to protect the upholstery from oil stains.

President Andrew Jackson poses with a walking stick for this 1832 portrait. Such sticks were handsome fashion accessories.

The French trendsetter Juliette Récamier (1777–1849) influenced women's fashion in Europe and America.

Chapter Six

STYLE SETTERS

Fashion icons in the Revolutionary and Victorian eras were wealthy women and men and those in the political limelight. American style setters included First Lady Dolley Madison. In Europe trendsetters included the French beauty Juliette Récamier and French empress Eugénie de Montijo (wife of Napoleon III).

Dolley Madison was born into the Quaker faith, which emphasizes simplicity. Yet Madison became the queen of society in Washington, D.C., and she dressed the part. A well-to-do woman, Mary Boardman Crowninshield, met Madison in 1815. She wrote this in a letter:

> She [Madison] was dressed in a white cambric [linen] gown, buttoned all the way up in front . . . ruffled around the bottom. A peach-bloom-colored scarf with a rich border over her shoulders. . . . She had on a spencer [short jacket] of satin of the same color, and likewise a turban of velour gauze, all of peach bloom. She looked very well indeed.

Englishman George "Beau" Brummell was the pioneer of fashion of his time. In this 1805 illustration, Brummell shows off his hat, tailcoat, boots, and elaborately tied cravat.

This letter also illustrates the way people learned about fashion in the days before television, photography, and the Internet. Few Americans would have actually seen Dolley Madison in person. They had to rely on letters from friends, newspaper articles, and other written accounts.

A MODEL FOR MEN

Englishman George Brummell (1778–1840) was nicknamed Beau, which means "handsome" in French. A close friend of Britain's Prince George (who later became King George IV), Brummell became famous in Great Britain for his stylish dress, his cleanliness, and his excellent manners. His style influenced Americans through fashion illustrations and by word of mouth. In fact, some fashion historians credit Brummell with almost single-handedly changing the style of European and American men's clothing.

Brummell turned tying a cravat into an art form. It was rumored that he had his gleaming boots cleaned with champagne. The Beau wore perfectly fitted cutaway coats and long trousers, made of fine wool and leather, in understated colors. His shirts were always snow white and crisply ironed.

Brummell's friend, Captain William Jesse, wrote of him, "He was a beau in the literal sense of the word,—'fine, handsome'.... His chief aim was to avoid anything marked [noticeable]; one of his aphorisms [sayings] being, that the severest mortification [embarrassment] a gentleman could incur, was, to attract observation in the street by his outward appearance."

This fashion doll, also known as a fashion baby, from the 1760s showed customers the fashions for spring, including a hooped skirt and a bonnet. Customers could use this doll as a guide to order clothing.

Fashion information came to the United States from Europe in several ways. American visitors to London and Paris brought back stylish new garments and accessories. Women also described clothing in letters to family and friends. In 1819 Rosalie Stier Calvert in Maryland wrote to her sister in Belgium, "Please send . . . several of those little engraved sketches showing morning and evening dress, like the ones you sent before—with them we will be able to copy your styles." Sometimes European dressmakers sent fashion babies to their customers in the United States. These were dolls outfitted in the latest styles. Customers used them as guides when ordering tailor-made clothing.

Both European and U.S. magazines included fashion plates, or illustrations. These hand-tinted prints showed men and women dressed in fashionable clothes. The most popular U.S. women's magazine was *Godey's Lady's Book*. Louis Godey of Philadelphia started the

Godey's Lady's Book featured colored illustrations, such as this one from an 1863 issue, of women's fashions. *Godey's Lady's Book* was the most popular magazine in the United States. The magazine was published until the late 1800s.

magazine in 1830. When Sarah Josepha Hale (author of "Mary Had a Little Lamb") became editor seven years later, the magazine soared in popularity. *Godey's* gave women advice on everything from proper behavior to furnishing their homes. Every issue featured these:

- **original poetry**
- **articles**
- **stories**, often by prominent writers of the day, such as Edgar Allan Poe, Nathaniel Hawthorne, and Oliver Wendell Holmes
- **engravings** by well-known artists
- **sheet music** for the piano

But *Godey's* was best known for its hand-tinted fashion plates. It also included clothing patterns with measurements for sewing garments at home. Similar periodicals, including the *Ladies' Companion, Graham's Magazine,* and *Peterson's Magazine*, began publishing later in the 1830s and in the 1840s.

This illustration from *Graham's Magazine* shows two fashionable women of the 1850s. *Graham's* was a popular American fashion magazine in the 1800s.

LIFE PASSAGES

For Revolutionary- and Victorian-era Americans, special occasions required special clothes, just as they do in modern times. For her wedding, a bride of these eras usually wore a new dress, but it wasn't just for the wedding. Most women continued to wear their wedding gowns for best—or important occasions—for a long time afterward.

One wealthy New Yorker wore a dress of green striped silk for her wedding in 1855. But like modern women, many Victorian-era brides wore white as a sign of purity. An 1856 *Godey's Lady's Book* fashion plate showed a wedding dress and came with this description:

> Dress of white silk, with three lace flounces . . . lace to correspond is also gathered in a slight fullness over the corsage [bosom], and falls over the open sleeve. Bouquets, wreath, and cordon of white roses, orange-flowers, and jassamine . . . veil of thulle [a sheer fabric], wide and full.

A man wore his best suit and hat at his wedding. He also continued to wear them for years afterward.

At a funeral, black was the proper color for both men and women. Then came a long period of mourning, during which a woman followed specific rules about clothing. If her husband had died, she was expected to wear mourning clothes for two years. For a dead mother, father, or child, mourning was worn for a year, and for grandparents and siblings, six months. The woman started out in full black and at certain points could transition to half-mourning, which meant she could wear gray and dull violet.

A bride wears her wedding gown in this 1850s photograph.

In these two daguerreotypes—one from the 1840s *(bottom)*, the other from the 1850s *(top)*—people dress in their best clothing.

The Wonderful DAGUERREOTYPE

In 1839 Frenchmen Louis Daguerre and Joseph Niépce invented the first workable photographic process. Daguerreotypes, as the resulting images were called, caught on fast. Photography studios sprang up all over the United States. As early as the 1840s, Americans were having their portraits taken, usually wearing their Sunday best. By 1860 the nation had more than three thousand professional photographers. People mailed their photographs to one another. These images of people dressed in their best clothing helped to spread fashion news.

This Confederate (Southern) private wears a homemade gray wool jacket and hat in 1863 during the Civil War. Around this time, the South ran out of manufactured gray dye and some uniforms turned a yellowy-tan color from the homemade mixture families had to use. Union (Northern) soldiers wore blue uniforms.

EPILOGUE

The Civil War was fought between Northern and Southern states, mostly over the issue of slavery. With the coming of war, the vigorous expansion and lively, hopeful spirit of the early 1800s came to an end, at least temporarily.

Men and boys by the thousands went off to war. In the North, many women took over running their family farms or their husbands' businesses. In the South, women also tried to hold their homes together and to run farms without husbands. The bulk of the fighting and the worst ravages of war took place in the South. Many Southern women tended to wounded soldiers and dealt with shortages of food and other necessities in their war-torn communities. For a time, practicality ruled. The extravagances of the latest fashions fell by the wayside.

When the war ended in 1865, Americans once again turned their attention to fun and fashion. The ready-made clothing industry grew larger and added women's clothing to the mix. More clothing shops opened in cities across the United States. People could even buy clothing by mail. They could look through catalogs filled with illustrations and descriptions, choose styles they liked, and have them delivered to their doors. And high-fashion clothing was no longer only for upper-and middle-class buyers. Working people, even the poor, could buy inexpensive—and stylish—ready-made clothing.

The 1897 Sears, Roebuck catalog sold these stylish boots by mail. Even working women could afford them.

When the Victorian era ended with the death of Queen Victoria in 1901, U.S. clothing began to change dramatically. Women began to wear shorter skirts and fewer petticoats. Eventually, women stopped wearing corsets. Men abandoned their waistcoats and detachable cuffs and collars. Before long, the only place to see pantaloons, breeches, and hoopskirts was at a historic costume exhibit.

Never *out of* Style

Most of the styles of the early United States are long gone. But they left a permanent mark on the history of fashion. For men, the tailored suit that replaced colonial knee breeches and frock coats lives on in modern times, with very little modification. Some early 1800s accessories—shoes with laces and leather wallets—remain fashion staples. And even small details, such as the tiny pocket just below the waistband of some men's pants, which once held a pocket watch, are still with us.

In the twenty-first century, the high-waisted, low-necked Empire-style dress is once again in style for women, although in a different form from the original. The bags, totes, and purses that modern women carry are direct descendants of the reticule. And ballet flats, descendants of early American women's slippers, are classic shoes that don't ever seem to go out of style. Who knows what other Revolutionary and early Victorian styles might come into fashion again? Cage crinolines? Top hats? Corsets? Only time will tell.

Some early-Victorian-era fashions have made a comeback. Award-winning actress Hilary Swank wears a corset to an awards banquet in 2010.

TIMELINE

1760s–1770s
Americans wear homespun and boycott fabrics made in Great Britain.

1775–1783
American colonists fight the Revolutionary War to gain independence from Great Britain.

1777
The Continental Congress adopts the Stars and Stripes, possibly created by upholsterer Betsy Ross, as the first American flag.

1778
Esther de Berdt Reed forms the Ladies of Philadelphia. With donated funds, the group buys linen and sews shirts for Continental Army soldiers.

1780
The first American hat factory opens in Danbury, Connecticut.

1789
The French Revolution begins in France. French people reject the elaborate fashions of the French court, and Americans soon follow suit. George Washington, the first U.S. president, wears an American-made woolen suit at his inauguration.

1790
In Rhode Island, Samuel Slater opens the first U.S. cotton mill, which operates by waterpower.

1793
Eli Whitney invents the cotton gin, a machine for separating cottonseeds from cotton fibers. This eventually allows manufacturers to produce cotton fabric in larger amounts and more quickly.

1800
Philadelphia boot maker William Young makes the first shoes specifically for the right and the left feet.

1814
In Massachusetts Francis Cabot Lowell opens the first factory to manufacture cloth from start to finish—from raw cotton to finished cloth.

1816 John Williams opens his Gentlemen's Fashionable Wearing Apparel Warehouse in New York City, one of the nation's first ready-made clothing stores.

1816 Henry Sands Brooks opens a tailoring shop in New York City (later called Brooks Brothers).

1823 Frenchman Antoine Gibus invents a collapsible top hat.

1830 Louis Godey, of Philadelphia, starts publishing *Godey's Lady's Book*, an influential women's and fashion magazine.

1837 Queen Victoria begins her reign in Great Britain, giving her name to the Victorian era. She greatly influences fashion in Europe and the United States.

1839 Louis Daguerre and Joseph Niépce invent the daguerreotype, a process for taking photographs. These photos provide an important record of period fashions.

1845 Elias Howe introduces the first practical sewing machine.

1851 Amelia Bloomer appears in public wearing baggy trousers (called bloomers) beneath her skirt. Isaac Singer patents an improved sewing machine.

1856 Women begin wearing cage crinolines instead of layered petticoats beneath their dresses.

1861–1865 Americans fight the Civil War, a conflict over whether the nation should allow slavery. Fashion becomes simple and practical.

1901 Queen Victoria dies, officially ending the Victorian era in Great Britain and the United States.

GLOSSARY

breeches: men's knee-length trousers, with a button front and knee bands, sometimes with buckles at the knee

chemise: a narrow one-piece dress with a high waist positioned just under the breasts, a low neckline, and very short puffed sleeves (also called an Empire-style dress). Sometimes shifts, plain sliplike undergarments worn beneath corsets, were also called chemises.

corset: a body-shaping woman's undergarment, boned for stiffness and tightened with laces. Corsets were called stays in the 1700s.

cravat: a long strip of white fabric, worn wrapped and knotted around a man's neck

drawers: knee-length underwear worn by women and men. Women's drawers were later called pantalets.

felt: matted fur or wool

frock coat: a skirted knee-length coat worn by men in the 1700s

homespun: a coarse but durable linen made from homegrown flax and cleaned, spun, and woven by women in their homes

linen: a fabric made from the flax plant

muslin: a fine, filmy, almost sheer cotton from India

petticoat: an underskirt worn beneath a dress or skirt

pocket: in the 1700s, a cloth sack tied around a woman's waist, under her skirt, in which she placed small personal items

reticule: a woman's small purse or handbag

shift: a plain linen garment, somewhat like a modern nightgown, worn beneath a corset as underwear; sometimes called a chemise

short gown: a short, boxy, loose-fitting woman's jacket

spencer: a woman's short, fitted jacket

tailcoat: a coat that flares open at the waist to form tails in back

tow: a coarse linen fabric made into clothing for slaves

tucker: a cloth with ruffles at the neck that tucks into the neckline of a woman's dress

waistcoat: a man's vest

5   Jack Larkin, *The Reshaping of Everyday Life,
    1790–1840* (New York: Harper Perennial,
    1989), 184–185.

6   Frances Milton Trollope, *Domestic Manners of
    the Americans* (1832; repr., London: Penguin
    Classics, 1997), 45–46.

7   Linda Baumgarten, *What Clothes Reveal: The
    Language of Clothing in Colonial Williamsburg
    and Federal America* (New Haven, CT: Colonial
    Williamsburg Foundation / Yale University
    Press, 2002), 132.

7   Ann Buermann Wass and Michelle Webb
    Fandrich, *Clothing through American History:
    The Federal Era through Antebellum, 1786–
    1860* (Santa Barbara, CA: Greenwood, 2010),
    124.

9   Michael Zakim, "Sartorial Ideologies: From
    Homespun to Ready-Made, *American
    Historical Review*, December 2001, http://
    www.historycooperative.org/journals/
    ahr/106.5/ah0501001553.html (March 25,
    2011).

14 Wass and Fandrich, *Clothing through
    American History*, 57.

15 Edward Warwick and Henry Pitz, "Early
    American Costume," AmericanRevolution.org,
    2010, www.americanrevolution.org/clothing/
    colonialclothing.html (March 25, 2011).

17 Stewart Mitchell, *New Letters of Abigail
    Adams: 1788–1801*, (Boston: Houghton
    Mifflin Company, 1947), 241–242.

17 Wass and Fandrich, *Clothing through
    American History*, 72.

17 Margaret Law Callcott, *Mistress of Riversdale:
    The Plantation Letters of Rosalie Stier Calvert
    1795–1821* (Baltimore: Johns Hopkins
    University Press, 1991), 77–78.

18 Sarah Jane Downing, *Fashion in the Time of
    Jane Austen* (Oxford, UK: Shire Publications,
    2010), 21.

19 Louisa May Alcott, *Little Women* (New York:
    Signet Classics, 2004), 92.

23 Wass and Fandrich, *Clothing through
    American History*, 148.

25 Ibid., 142.

25 Trollope, Domestic Manners, 116.

25 Michael Zakim, *Ready-Made Democracy:
    A History of Men's Dress in the American
    Republic, 1760–1860* (Chicago: University of
    Chicago Press, 2003), 192.

26 Ibid., 194.

27 Wass and Fandrich, *Clothing through
    American History*, 372.

28 R.L. Shep, ed., *The Ladies' Self Instructor in
    Millinery and Mantua Making, Embroidery
    and Applique* (1853; repr., Fort Bragg, CA: R.
    L. Shep, 1988), 132.

28 Zakim, *Ready-Made*, 181.

29 Larkin, *Reshaping of Everyday Life*, 27.

30 Trollope, *Domestic Manners*, 42.

30 Wilder, Laura Ingalls. *Little House in the Big
    Woods*, Harper & Row, Publishers, New York,
    170

32 Zakim, *Ready-Made*, 97–98.

SOURCE NOTES

32 Ibid., 207.

33 Wass and Fandrich, *Clothing through American History*, 372.

35 Louisa May Alcott, *Little Women* (New York: Signet Classics, 2004), 85.

37 Zakim, *Ready-Made*, 181.

38 Gwen Raverat, *Period Piece: A Cambridge Childhood* (London: Faber and Faber, 1970), 260.

39 Callcott, *Mistress of Riversdale*, 80.

39 Trollope, *Domestic Manners*, 233.

40 Ibid., 260.

42 Sharon Ann Burnston, *Fitting and Proper: 18th Century Clothing from the Collection of the Chester County Historical Society* (Texarkana, TX: Scurlock Publishing Co., 1998), 100.

44 Baumgarten, *What Clothes Reveal*, 90.

46 Wass and Fandrich, *Clothing through American History*, 80.

47 Ibid.

48 Captain William Jesse, *The Life of George Brummell, Esq., Commonly Called Beau Brummel*, vol. 1 (London: Saunders and Otley, Contuit Street, 1844), 59.

48 Callcott, *Mistress of Riverdale*, 346–347.

50 Ellen M. Plante, *Women at Home in Victorian America: A Social History* (New York: Facts on File, 1997), 22.

SELECTED BIBLIOGRAPHY

Alcott, Louisa May. *Little Women*. New York: Signet Classics, 2004.

American Textile History Museum. "Costume." American Textile History Museum, N.d. http://www.athm.org/collections/costume/ (March 2, 2011).

Baumgarten, Linda. *What Clothes Reveal: The Language of Clothing in Colonial Williamsburg and Federal America*. New Haven, CT: Colonial Williamsburg Foundation / Yale University Press, 2002.

Boston University Libraries. "Clothing, Fashion, and Appearance." Boston University Libraries Research Guides, N.d. http://www.bu.edu/library/guides/clothing.html (March 1, 2011).

Bunkers, Susanne L., ed. *Diaries of Girls and Women: A Midwestern Sampler*. Madison: University of Wisconsin Press, 2001.

Burnston, Sharon Ann. *Fitting and Proper: 18th Century Clothing from the Collection of the Chester County Historical Society*. Texarkana, TX: Scurlock Publishing Co., 1998.

Callcott, Margaret Law. *Mistress of Riversdale: The Plantation Letters of Rosalie Stier Calvert 1795–1821*. Baltimore: Johns Hopkins University Press, 1991.

Colonial Williamsburg. "Historic Threads: Three Centuries of Clothing." Colonial Williamsburg, 2011. http://www.history.org/history/museums/clothingexhibit/index.cfm (March 1, 2011).

Dalrymple, Priscilla Harris. *American Victorian Costume in Early Photographs*. New York: Dover Publications, 1991.

De Pauw, Linda Grant. *Remember the Ladies: Women in America 1750–1815*. New York: Viking Press, 1976.

Downing, Sarah Jane. *Fashion in the Time of Jane Austen*. Oxford, UK: Shire Publications, 2010.

Forest, Jennifer. *Jane Austen's Sewing Box: Craft Projects and Stories from Jane Austen's Novels*. Miller's Point, New South Wales, Australia: Murdoch Books Pty., 2009.

Larkin, Jack. *The Reshaping of Everyday Life*, 1790–1840. New York: Harper Perennial, 1989.

Metropolitan Museum of Art. "Works of Art: The Costume Institute." Metropolitan Museum of Art. 2000–2011. http://www.metmuseum.org/Works_of_Art/department.asp?dep=8 (March 1, 2011).

Mitchell, Stewart. *New Letters of Abigail Adams: 1788–1801*. Boston: Houghton Mifflin Company, 1947.

Plante, Ellen M. *Women at Home in Victorian America: A Social History*. New York: Facts on File, 1997.

Raverat, Gwen. *Period Piece: A Cambridge Childhood*. London: Faber and Faber Limited, 1970.

Shep, R.L., ed. *The Ladies' Self Instructor in Millinery and Mantua Making, Embroidery and Appliqué*. 1853. Reprint, Fort Bragg, CA: R. L. Shep, 1988.

Smithsonian National Museum of American History. "Costume Collection, Women's Dresses." Smithsonian National Museum of American History, N.d. http://americanhistory.si.edu/collections/costume/ (March 1, 2011).

Trollope, Frances Milton. *Domestic Manners of the Americans*. 1832. Reprint, London: Penguin Classics, 1997.

Warwick, Edward, and Henry Pitz, "Early American Costume." AmericanRevolution.org. 2010. http://www.americanrevolution.org/clothing/colonialclothing.html (March 1, 2011).

Wass, Ann Buermann, and Michelle Webb Fandrich. *Clothing through American History: The Federal Era through Antebellum, 1786–1860*. Santa Barbara, CA: Greenwood, 2010.

Wilcox, R. Turner. *Five Centuries of American Costume*. New York: Macmillan Publishing Company, 1963.

Zakim, Michael. *Ready-Made Democracy: A History of Men's Dress in the American Republic, 1760–1860*. Chicago: University of Chicago Press, 2003.

FURTHER READING, WEBSITES, AND FILMS

BOOKS

Bunkers, Susanne L., ed. *Diaries of Girls and Women: A Midwestern Sampler*. Madison: University of Wisconsin Press, 2001.
Not specifically about clothing, this book looks into the lives of U.S. girls and women during the 1800s.

Hoobler, Dorothy, and Thomas Hoobler. *Vanity Rules: A History of American Fashion and Beauty*. Minneapolis: Twenty-First Century Books, 2000.
This book takes a lively look at men's and women's fashion, hairstyles, and other beauty topics.

Miller, Marie Brandon. *Declaring Independence: Life during the American Revolution*. Minneapolis: Twenty-First Century Books, 2005.
This fascinating title in the People's History series examines life during the American Revolution, not just for soldiers and political leaders but for ordinary men, women, and children.

———. *Dressed for the Occasion: What Americans Wore 1620–1970*. Minneapolis: Lerner Publications Company, 1999.
Miller offers interesting facts about the history of U.S. clothing for both men and women. The text is illustrated with vintage photographs and paintings.

———. *Growing Up in Revolution and the New Nation 1775 to 1800*. Minneapolis: Lerner Publications, 2002.
Learn more about what life was like for young people in the early history of U.S. nationhood, including what they wore.

Riley, Mara. *Whatever Shall I Wear? A Guide to Assembling a Woman's Basic 18th Century Wardrobe*. Excelsior Springs, MO: Graphics/Fine Arts Press, 2002.
Written for costumers and historical reenactors, this illustrated guide shows how to create, in accurate detail, typical eighteenth-century women's clothing and hairstyles.

Shaskan, Kathy. *How Underwear Got Under There: A Brief History*. New York: Dutton Children's Books, 2007.
This picture book takes a humorous look at the history of underwear, including some bizarre underwear fads.

WEBSITES

American Textile History Museum, Costume Collection
http://www.athm.org/collections/costume/
The museum's Costume Collection includes garments worn by Americans from the eighteenth through the twentieth centuries. The focus is on everyday clothing items and stories of the people who owned them.

Colonial Williamsburg, Historic Threads: Three Centuries of Clothing
http://www.history.org/history/museums/clothingexhibit/index.cfm
This exhibit from Colonial Williamsburg in Virginia, a living history museum, includes excellent examples of American colonial clothing.

Costume Society of America
http://www.costumesocietyamerica.com/
This organization collects information on and images of clothing from collections all over the world, from every era. The website features many of these images.

Daughters of the American Revolution Museum
http://www.dar.org/museum/
Museum exhibits and programs often feature clothing from the organization's excellent costume collection.

Metropolitan Museum of Art, Costume Institute
http://www.metmuseum.org/Works_of_Art/
department.asp?dep=8
The Costume Institute has one of the world's best collections of costumes and accessories from various eras. Many costumes can be viewed online.

Smithsonian National Museum of American History, Costume Collection
http://americanhistory.si.edu/collections/costume/
The online collection includes clothing from the Revolutionary and early Victorian periods. The museum also has an exhibit of clothing worn by first ladies.

FILMS

John Adams. DVD. New York: HBO Films, 2008.
This seven-part TV miniseries chronicles the life of John Adams, the second president of the United States. Paul Giamatti stars as Adams, with Laura Linney as his wife, Abigail. The actors dress in period-specific costumes, showing how ordinary citizens, soldiers, and ladies and gentlemen dressed in Adams's era.

Little Women. DVD. Culver City, CA: Columbia Pictures Corporation, 1994.
One of several film adaptations of the classic novel by Louisa May Alcott, this movie tells the story of the March sisters. It also shows how young women dressed in New England in the mid-1800s. Stars include Winona Ryder, Susan Sarandon, Gabriel Byrne, Kirsten Dunst, Claire Danes, and Christian Bale.

LERNER
SOURCE

Expand learning beyond the printed book. Download free, complementary educational resources for this book from our website, www.lerneresource.com.

INDEX

ABOUT THE AUTHOR

Cynthia Overbeck Bix grew up in Baltimore, Maryland. Family visits to historical sites, including Old Sturbridge Village, Colonial Williamsburg, and Baltimore's own Fort McHenry, sparked her early interest in American history, crafts, and everyday life.

Now living in the San Francisco Bay area, Cynthia loves to write about anything and everything. In her more than thirty nonfiction books for children and adults, she has written about such diverse subjects as fine art, natural science, and domestic arts. She has also written how-to-do-it books about all kinds of activities, from making impressions of animal footprints to planting a garden. In addition to writing, Cynthia edits books for both children and adults.

PHOTO ACKNOWLEDGMENTS